I0002290

\

THE SMARTPHONE
TITANS

Examine the qualities of the Samsung Galaxy S24 and iPhone 15, weigh the benefits and drawbacks, and select the best.

Adrian Zims

All rights reserved. No part of this publication may be reproduced, distributed, or transmitted in any form or by any means, including photocopying, recording, or other electronic or mechanical methods, without the prior written permission of the publisher, except in the case of brief quotations embodied in critical reviews and specific other noncommercial uses permitted by copyright law.
Copyright © Adrian Zims, 2024.

Contents

Introduction

In just a few decades, smartphones have experienced a remarkable metamorphosis, going from bulky brick phones with simple messaging and calling features to sleek, multipurpose gadgets that are effectively computers on a smaller scale. A look into their intriguing trip may be found here:

Early Years (1973–1990s): 1973 saw the invention of the Motorola DynaTAC 8000X, the first mobile phone. It had a substantial 2.4 kg weight and a meager 30-minute talk time.

1983: At a pricey $3,995, the DynaTAC 8000x, the first mobile phone to be sold commercially, is released.

1989 saw the release of the Motorola MicroTAC, the first flip phone with enhanced mobility and design.

Smartphones' Early Years (1990s–2000s):

1992 saw the release of the Simon Personal Communicator by IBM, which is regarded as the original smartphone. It had an address book and calendar in addition to email functionality and a touchscreen.

1997: Ericsson introduces the word "smartphone" to refer to their GS88 phone, initiating a trend toward gadgets with sophisticated features and functionalities.

2000 saw the arrival of the first camera phone, the Kyocera VP6010, which let users take and share pictures while they were on the road.

2001: Smartphones become internet-enabled, providing a plethora of opportunities for email, surfing, and even the development of early mobile apps.

Powerhouses' Ascent (2007-Present):

2007: With the release of the first iPhone, which had a large touchscreen, an easy-to-use interface, and a vast app store, Apple transformed the market.

2008 saw the release of the open-source Android operating system, which sparked an explosion of varied and reasonably priced smartphone alternatives from different producers.

2010s: With enhanced CPUs, bigger, sharper screens, sophisticated cameras, and fresh features like fingerprint sensors and face recognition, smartphones becoming more and more potent.

The 2020s: Foldable screens, 5G connection, artificial intelligence integration, and an emphasis on wellness and health features are examples of how smartphone innovation is continuing.

The Value of Selecting the Correct Smartphone

Choosing the best smartphone these days might be daunting due to the wide variety of options available. However, you must make a well-informed choice based on your unique requirements and preferences. These are some necessities to consider:

Which operating system, iOS or Android? Each has advantages and disadvantages of its own, so take your preferred user experience and app compatibility into account.

Budget: The cost of smartphones varies, ranging from low-cost to high-end. Establish your spending limit and rank the things that are most essential to you.

Screen Size and Resolution: Select a screen size and resolution that will provide a pleasant viewing experience based on how you want to use your phone (gaming, streaming, etc.).

Camera Quality: How many pictures and movies do you take each day? If so, give the megapixel count, characteristics of the lens, and low-light capability top priority.

Battery Life: For frequent users, a phone with a long battery life is vital. Seek gadgets having powerful batteries and effective CPUs.

Processor and RAM: These determine the general performance and task-handling capacity of your phone. Select specifications based on your intended use.

Storage: Take into account the amount of space you require for music, movies, pictures, and apps. Choose extendable storage if you think you'll need extra room in the future.

Design and Durability: Do outdoor activities require a robust phone? Take water resistance and construction quality into account. Additionally, pick a design that suits your taste in style.

You may select a smartphone that best suits your lifestyle and makes the most of your mobile experience by giving these things considerable thought. Recall that there isn't a single characteristic that works for everyone, so rank the attributes that are most important to you first and do your homework to identify the best match.

Chapter 1: Preview of the iPhone 15

Apple's flagship smartphone portfolio took an exciting stride ahead with the release of the iPhone 15, which was released in late 2023. It brought about several notable improvements in terms of design, display, camera, and performance, all while maintaining the iconic iPhone DNA. Let's examine the specifics:

Create & Construct:

Sturdy and Colorful: With an aerospace-grade aluminum frame and color-infused rear glass, the iPhone 15 has a sleek and robust design. In comparison to earlier versions, this new "DuraGlass" claims considerably greater scratch and fracture resistance. Five vivid colors are available for the phone: Pink, Yellow, Green, Blue, and Black.

Slightly Larger Sizes: The screens of the iPhone 15 and 15 Plus are marginally bigger than those of their predecessors. The Super Retina XDR display of the iPhone 15 is 6.1 inches, and the 15 Plus has a 6.7-inch display.

Technology of Displays:

Smoother and Brighter: With a peak brightness of up to 1200 nits, the Super Retina XDR screens are more brilliant than ever, improving outdoor visibility. Additionally, they provide ultra-smooth 120Hz refresh rates for a more responsive and pleasurable experience on Pro models thanks to support for ProMotion technology.

Dynamic Island: The front-facing camera and Face ID sensors are housed in the "Dynamic Island," a pill-shaped notch that replaces the conventional notch on the iPhone 15. This creative design minimizes distractions and presents fresh methods to engage with alerts and notifications while blending in perfectly with the display.

Features of the iPhone 15 Dynamic Island Camera:

Pro-Grade Improvements: The cameras on the iPhone 15 Pro models represent a major advancement in technology. Their new 48-megapixel primary sensor is a major improvement over the old 12-megapixel sensor. This enables the capture of remarkably detailed images and films with enhanced low-light capabilities.

Improvements to the telephoto lenses are another feature of the Pro versions; the 15 Pro Max has a 5x optical zoom, while the 15 Pro has a 3x optical zoom. This improves your capacity to take very clear pictures of far-off subjects.

Improvements to the Cinematic Mode: The Pro models now offer 4K HDR recording, which significantly enhances your filmmaking talents.

The Cinematic Mode adds creative depth-of-field blurring to recordings.

Processor and Performance:

A16 Bionic processor: The A16 Bionic processor, which offers notable performance enhancements over the A15 Bionic, powers the iPhone 15 and 15 Pro. This results in improved gaming experiences, seamless multitasking, and quicker app loads.

Better Battery Life: Apple claims that the iPhone 15 and 15 Plus have better batteries, with the former lasting up to 26 hours and the latter up to 29 hours. This is attributable to both the higher battery capacity and the more efficient A16 chip.

iOS (operating system):

operates on the most recent version of iOS 17, which has a polished user experience with enhanced customization choices, accessibility features, and multitasking.

close integration with additional Apple products and services to create a smooth environment. Access to new features and reliable performance are guaranteed by frequent software upgrades.

Special Qualities:

Dynamic Island: A pill-shaped cutout that houses the Face ID sensors and front-facing camera takes the place of the notch. To present notifications, warnings, and Live Activities in a visually appealing manner, this dynamic interface extends and adapts.

Always-On Display: The iPhone 15 Pro minimizes the need to repeatedly wake the smartphone by displaying important information including the time, date, and alerts even while the screen is off.

Satellite Connectivity: Available in some locations, Emergency SOS via satellite enables contact in distant areas without cellular service.

Advantages:

superior functionality and camera capabilities.

superior construction and design quality.

smooth interaction with the Apple environment.

Extended security support and routine software upgrades.

The user experience is improved by special features like Always-On Display and Dynamic Island.

Cons:

Greater cost in comparison to other brands.
fewer personalization choices than phones running Android.

Some users may find it inconvenient as there is no headphone jack or expandable storage.

Open-source Android users may find a closed ecosystem to be too constraining.

All things considered, the iPhone 15 offers an alluring combination of performance, power, and cutting-edge features. It is still a strong option for those looking for the greatest Apple experience to date, despite its high price and limited environment.

Chapter 2: Samsung Galaxy S24

Preview of the Samsung Galaxy S24: Three Models, Major Upgrades

Three models comprise the Samsung Galaxy S24 series, which was introduced in January 2024:

S24: 6.2-inch screen, 128GB or 256GB of storage, 8GB of RAM.

S24 Plus: 256GB of storage, 8GB of RAM, and a 6.7-inch display.

S24 Ultra: 6.8-inch screen, 256GB, 512GB, or 1TB of storage, 12GB of RAM.

Here's a succinct summary of the main attributes:

Create & Construct:

In comparison to their predecessors, all models feature bigger screens and thinner bezels.

Elegant style, available in a range of colors, including aluminum frames and glass backs.

The Ultra's boxier form and integrated S Pen stylus make it stand out.

Technology of Displays:

Dynamic AMOLED 2X panels with 120Hz refresh rates are a feature of all models, allowing for incredibly fluid scrolling and images.

The Ultra has a Quad HD+ display, while the S24 and S24 Plus have Full HD+ resolution.

With the S24 Plus and Ultra, peak brightness reaches an impressive 2600 nits, guaranteeing exceptional visibility even in direct sunshine.

Features of the camera:

All versions include triple-lens rear camera systems, but the Ultra pushes the envelope with a 200MP primary sensor.

Enhanced low-light performance and scene optimization are driven by AI for beautiful images and videos under any kind of illumination.

With its two telephoto lenses (one optical and one digital), the Ultra has remarkable zoom powers.

All versions have a 12MP front-facing camera for clear video calls and selfies.

Processor and Performance:

The most recent Snapdragon 8 Gen 3 CPU powers all models, providing excellent performance for taxing activities and multitasking.

Fast file transfers and app loading are guaranteed by the S24 Plus and Ultra's UFS 4.0 storage.

For consumers needing more power for intensive tasks, the Ultra has the highest RAM (12GB).

Android operating system:

Samsung's One UI 5.1 overlays with the most recent version of Android 13, providing a flexible and easy-to-use interface with simple navigation.

Several choices for customizing apps and access to the extensive Google Play Store network.
Updated software guarantees enhanced security and new feature availability.

Special Qualities:

AMOLED screens with a refresh rate of 120 Hz: All models have bright, colorful displays that are incredibly responsive.

Improved camera systems: The S24 Ultra and S24+ have superior cameras with more megapixels, better low-light performance, and more powerful zoom.

Integration with S Pen: For creative work, taking notes, and fine control, the S24 Ultra is compatible with the S Pen stylus.

AI-powered features: For a more customized experience, Samsung's AI engine optimizes battery life, performance, and camera settings.

Advantages:

Excellent performance is provided by powerful Exynos 2400 or Snapdragon 8 Gen 3 CPUs.

Gorgeous AMOLED screens with refreshing refresh rates of 120 Hz.

Adaptable camera systems with outstanding quality for both photos and videos (particularly on S24 Ultra).

The open Android ecosystem provides a wide range of app options and customization settings. robust batteries that can be quickly charged.

The S Pen integration on S24 Ultra gives a special tool for creativity and productivity.

Cons:

More expensive than some of its rivals.

Some consumers who want a clean Android experience might find Samsung's One UI overlay to be overly complex.

The regular S24's plastic back may not feel as high-end as other models' glass backs.

When compared to earlier versions, the increase in battery life is apparent but not very noteworthy.

All things considered, the Samsung Galaxy S24 series is a big improvement over its predecessors and is suitable for a broad spectrum of customers. With its flagship specifications and S Pen experience, the Ultra pushes the boundaries, while the S24 is a good all-arounder and the S24 Plus has a larger screen and more storage.

Chapter 3:Analogous Comparison

Titans of the smartphone market, the iPhone 15 and Samsung Galaxy S24 are always pushing the envelope in terms of design and technology. But it might be difficult to decide between them when they are such strong competitors. Let's compare and contrast their salient characteristics so you can determine which is best for your requirements.

Create & Construct:

The iPhone 15 boasts an aerospace-grade metal frame and a color-infused rear glass, giving it a sleek and minimalistic appearance. In five vivid hues. Pink, Yellow, Green, Blue, and Black—for your choice.

Samsung Galaxy S24: Features a matte metal frame, a gently curved back, and an elegant, contemporary style. available in four high-end hues, including Bora Purple, Mystic Green, Silver, and Phantom Black.

Quality of Display:

The iPhone 15 features a 6.1-inch Super Retina XDR OLED display with True Tone technology for the best possible color accuracy and a peak brightness of 2000 nits. The refresh rate is still 60Hz, though, as opposed to the S24's smoother 120Hz.

The Samsung Galaxy S24 boasts a bigger 6.2-inch Dynamic AMOLED 2X display with a refresh rate of 120Hz, resulting in very smooth animations and scrolling. It is even brighter than the iPhone 15 with a peak brightness of 2600 nits.

Camera Features:

With its 48MP primary sensor and 12MP ultra-wide sensor, the iPhone 15 boasts a dual-camera setup that produces amazing images and movies in most lighting circumstances. Professional-style depth-of-field effects are added with 4K HDR's cinematic mode.

The Samsung Galaxy S24 is equipped with three cameras: a 12MP ultra-wide sensor, a 10MP telephoto lens with an optical zoom of three times, and a 50MP primary sensor. Other benefits include better Night Mode photography and Super Slow-mo video capture at 960 frames per second.

Performance metrics for the Samsung Galaxy S24 camera:

iPhone 15: Equipped with an A16 Bionic CPU, this device offers unparalleled speed and processing capacity for intensive workloads and multitasking. Smooth performance is ensured by 6GB of RAM.

With the most recent Snapdragon 8 Gen 3 CPU, the Samsung Galaxy S24 has a performance that is similar to that of the A16 Bionic chip. Heavy users may choose between RAM versions of 8GB or 12 GB.

Comparing Operating Systems:

iOS 17: Provides enhanced customizing choices, accessibility features, and a more polished user experience with better multitasking. A seamless ecosystem is produced by close connection with other Apple products and services. The two biggest benefits are longer security support and regular software upgrades.

Android 13: Offers open-source freedom and a highly customized experience. provides more control over device settings and a broader range of app compatibility. On the other hand, fragmentation across phone makers may be a problem and upgrades may be delayed.

Showdown of Special Features:

iPhone 15: Interactive alerts and a more immersive display are provided by Dynamic Island, which takes the place of the notch. The iPhone 15 Plus's Always-On Display keeps important information visible even while the screen is off. Satellite-based emergency SOS communication enables contact in far-flung locations without cellphone service.

Samsung Galaxy S24: A stylish and practical way to unlock the device is using the under-display fingerprint sensor. A built-in S Pen stylus improves creativity and productivity (on certain models only). Precise device sharing and location tracking are made possible by ultra-wideband technologies.

The Samsung Galaxy S24 and iPhone 15 are both superb smartphones, each having advantages and disadvantages of its own. The optimal option ultimately relies on your personal preferences and priorities.

Select the iPhone 15 in light of its superior performance, smooth integration with the Apple ecosystem, frequent software updates, exceptional camera performance in most lighting conditions, and special features like Dynamic Island and Always-On Display (available only on the Plus model).

The Samsung Galaxy S24 is a great option if you want a smoother 120Hz display, a more flexible triple-camera setup with a telephoto lens, a very configurable Android experience, and cutting-edge technologies like an under-display fingerprint sensor and ultra-wideband technology.

Recall that there is no incorrect response! To make the best decision for your tech adventure, take into account your operating system preference, required features, and budget.

Chapter 4: User Interface

The final decision between the Samsung Galaxy S24 and the iPhone 15 comes down to personal taste in terms of user interface. Both are quite capable, yet they are best in distinct domains:

A. User-Friendliness and Interface:

iPhone 15: iOS 17 emphasizes simplicity and ease of use with a clear and user-friendly interface. Because gestures are often dependable and constant, navigating is easy and effective. Apple places a high value on the user experience, making it easy for even beginners to get started.

Samsung Galaxy S24: With themes, widgets, and icon packs, One UI 5.1 on the S24 provides further visual customization choices. Because of all of its features and options, it has a slightly longer learning curve, but power users who like to customize their experience will like the versatility.

App Environment:

iPhone 15: Better stability and performance are often the result of the App Store's carefully chosen collection of premium apps with more stringent App Review policies. Some specialized apps, nevertheless, could initially be accessible on Android.

Google Play Store provides a greater selection of apps, some of which are unavailable on iOS, for the Samsung Galaxy S24. On the other hand, there may be more bloatware and more variation in app quality.

Customization Possibilities:

iPhone 15: Compared to Android, iOS customization choices are more restricted. Although some customizing is possible through wallpapers and widgets, more system-level customization is not offered.

Samsung Galaxy S24: The One UI offers a great deal of customization, such as settings for always-on display, custom icons, app drawer organization, and themes. Because Android is open-source, third-party launchers and customizations are possible for even more customization.

Characteristics of Accessibility:

Strong accessibility features including Zoom magnification, VoiceOver screen reader, and Switch Control for one-handed operation are included on the iPhone 15 and iOS 17. Apple is a leader in accessibility and places a high priority on it.

Comprehensive accessibility features including a TalkBack screen reader, Bixby voice assistant, and one-handed operating mode are also available on the Samsung Galaxy S24: One UI. In this aspect, both phones shine.

Depending on your priorities, you can choose between the Samsung Galaxy S24 and the iPhone 15:

Ease of use and simplicity: The iPhone 15 impresses with its well-organized app store and simple layout.

Flexibility and customization: S24 provides a greater selection of apps along with a plethora of customizing choices.

Accessibility: With features that meet a variety of demands, both phones excel in accessibility.

In the end, you might try both phones if you can to determine which features and interface appeal to you the most. While they serve distinct tastes, both provide excellent user experiences.

Chapter 5: Life of Batteries and Charging

iPhone 15 battery capacity: 3,349 mAh for the base model and 4,200 mAh for the Plus variant. Samsung Galaxy S24: the normal model has 4,000mAh, while the Plus variant has 4,900mAh.

Technologies for Charging:

iPhone 15: Wired charging: Takes around 30 minutes to reach 50% charge, and may reach a maximum of 25W with a suitable adaptor.

Wireless charging: Up to 15W of MagSafe and 7.5W of Qi wireless charging are supported.

Samsung Galaxy S24: Wired charging: reaches 50% in around 30 minutes with the Plus model; up to 45W with a suitable adapter (not provided in the package).

Wireless power sharing and Fast Wireless Charging 2.0 with a maximum power of 15W are supported.

Battery capacity: The basic versions of the Galaxy S24 include a bigger battery that may provide longer battery life.

Faster charging (up to 45W vs. 25W) is possible with the Galaxy S24 when charging by wire, however an additional adaptor is needed.

Wireless charging: The 15W wireless charging speeds offered by both are comparable.

Actual battery life: The iPhone 15 is renowned for its effective software and optimization, which results in remarkable battery life even with a lower capacity. The Galaxy S24, on the other hand, has a bigger battery. To compare their real-world usage time definitively, extensive assessments will be required.

Other Things to Think About

Screen size and resolution: Larger, higher-resolution screens tend to use up batteries more quickly.

User behavior: Demanding activities like gaming and streaming use greater battery life.
Connectivity: Using cellular data uses more battery life than using Wi-Fi.

Software optimization: Although individual outcomes may differ, both manufacturers tune their software for battery life.

The iPhone 15's smaller battery and slower charging may not result in a noticeably reduced battery life because of its optimized software, even if the Galaxy S24 has a bigger battery and faster cable charging. With typical use, most users should have plenty of battery life with both phones. The optimal option ultimately relies on your preferences and use habits. When making your choice, take into account all the variables and refer to thorough evaluations.

Chapter 6: Interactions

Although the Galaxy S24 and iPhone 15 both have excellent connectivity choices, there are a few important distinctions to take into account: cellular

Both: Take advantage of 5G networks for fast data transfers and reduced latency.

Galaxy S24: Depending on the market variation, this smartphone could support more 5G bands in specific areas.

WiFi:

The iPhone 15 is outfitted with Wi-Fi 7, the most recent version that provides enhanced latency and potential speeds over 30 Gbps.

Galaxy S24: Offers multi-gigabit speeds and less interference in the 6 GHz band, and it supports Wi-Fi 6E.

Bluetooth:

Both: Provide enhanced audio quality, reduced battery consumption, and increased connectivity range by supporting the most recent Bluetooth 5.3 standard.

Additional Disparities:

USB Port: iPhone 15: Eventually adopts USB-C, although data transfer is limited to 480 Mbps and only supports USB 2 rates.

The Galaxy S24 boasts much higher data transfer speeds of up to 10 Gbps and uses USB-C with full compatibility for USB 3.2 Gen 2.

Satellite connectivity is available on the iPhone 15, however it is presently only available in a few locales. It allows emergency SOS messages to be sent in distant locations without cellular service.

As of right now, there is no verified data on satellite connectivity for Galaxy S24.

Ability:

iPhone 15: Smooth file sharing with other Apple devices thanks to close interaction with Apple services and AirDrop.

Galaxy S24: To simulate a desktop, connect the device to an external monitor or display using Samsung DeX mode.

Both: Provide support for many media streaming protocols and mobile payment systems such as Samsung Pay and Apple Pay.

As a whole:

iPhone 15: With Wi-Fi 7 and emergency satellite communication, it's future-proofed, but its slow USB 2 speeds restrict it.

Galaxy S24: Flexibility is provided by wide 5G band compatibility, quicker USB 3.2 transfers, and the possibility of desktop-like features.

Your demands will determine which connectivity is best for you.

Regular file transfers: USB-C is quicker on the Galaxy S24.

Preemptive innovation and early access to cutting-edge technologies: the Wi-Fi 7 feature of the iPhone 15 may be enticing.

When visiting distant locations, look for emergency satellite functions, which are now offered in some places on the iPhone 15.

In the end, both phones provide a wide range of connectivity possibilities; the optimal decision will rely on your own preferences and usage habits.

Chapter 7: Value for Cost and Prices

The Samsung Galaxy S24 and the iPhone 15 might be chosen based on personal objectives and financial constraints. They both have great features, but their prices and extra expenses are different, which affects the total value of the money.

Base Model Cost:

iPhone 15: 128GB storage starts at $799.

Samsung Galaxy S24: 128GB storage starts at $899.

Extra Expenses:

Upgrading storage on the iPhone 15 costs $899 for 256GB and $1099 for 512 GB.

Samsung Galaxy S24: $849 for 256GB, $949 for 512GB.

Accessory: Cases, chargers, and headphones are among the many official and third-party accessories that are available for both phones, and their prices are comparable.

Warranty: The phones from both manufacturers come with regular one-year warranties. For a fee, extended warranties with accidental damage protection are offered by Samsung Care+ and AppleCare+.

Worth for Money:

The advantages of the iPhone 15 include its unmatched speed, excellent camera quality, easy connection with the Apple ecosystem, frequent software upgrades, and increased security support.

Cons: Expensive starting price, few storage options, lack of headphone jack or extendable storage, restricted ecosystem.

Value: Outstanding for customers who are prepared to spend more on the Apple ecosystem, performance, and camera.

Advantages of the Samsung Galaxy S24 include its competitive pricing, smoother 120Hz display, more storage possibilities, expandable storage, open Android environment, and special features like compatibility with the S Pen.

Cons: Less regular software upgrades; somewhat worse camera quality than the iPhone 15.

Value: Outstanding for customers who value low costs, a fluid display, adaptable storage, and an open Android environment.

As a whole:
Depending on your preferences, both phones are affordable. The iPhone 15's higher price is justified if performance, camera quality, and the Apple ecosystem are your top priorities. The Galaxy S24 is a fantastic option if price, display, storage capacity, and the open Android environment are your top priorities.

Value in the Long Run:

Software upgrades: Android upgrades are dependent on phone carriers and manufacturers, however, Apple usually offers extended software support for older iPhone models. The iPhone 15 may continue to get upgrades.

Resale Value: If you intend to upgrade later, the iPhone 15 could be a better investment because iPhones often maintain their resale value better than Android phones.

Cost of Repairs and Durability: Although both are constructed with sturdy materials, iPhone repairs might be more costly. Think about available warranties and possible repair expenses.

The best value for your money ultimately comes down to your priorities and demands. To make an informed choice, think about the features and ecosystem you want, budget first, and account for resale value and long-term software support.

Chapter 8: Summary and Suggestion

The verdict: For fans of iOS and Apple products: With its flawless entry into the Apple ecosystem, consistent software updates, and unparalleled performance for iOS apps, the iPhone 15 is the clear winner. The dynamic island and always-on display, among other exclusive features, improve the user experience even more.

For value-seekers and aficionados of Android: Particularly in some areas, the Samsung Galaxy S24 provides a possibly better value for money together with a more customized UI and open environment. For some, its longer battery life, expanded storage, and better display will be crucial features.

Suggestion:
Select the iPhone 15 if: You value easy compatibility with other Apple products.
Better performance for iOS apps is important to you.

You value special features such as Always-On Display and Dynamic Island.

You value regular software upgrades and ongoing security assistance.

Select the Samsung Galaxy S24 if: You value Android's adaptability and customizability.
Cost-effectiveness is a key consideration.

Longer battery life, an extendable storage capacity, and a brighter display are characteristics you like.

You are drawn to a more expansive app selection and an open ecosystem.

The optimal option ultimately relies on your requirements and preferences. Compare your priorities with each phone's advantages and disadvantages. Before making your choice, read reviews and get first-hand experience to gain a better grasp of their features and user interface.

An overview of the main variations: feature iPhone 15 Android 13. iOS 17 Samsung Galaxy S24 Operating System

Present6.1" or 6.7" 120Hz Super Retina XDRAMOLED 6.2" (120Hz)

A16 Bionic Snapdragon 8 Gen 3 Processor Snapshot50MP plus 12MP + 10MP back, 12MP front, 48MP + 12MP dual rear, 12MP front.

Specialty FeaturesAlways-On Display, Dynamic Island (Pro models)Support for S Pens and Dex desktop mode.

Keepsake256, 512, and 128 GB (non-expandable)256, 512, and 128 GB (expandable).

Life of Battery20 hours or more of video playback28 hours or more of video playback Pricing begins at $799 and ends at $699.

Suggestions from the Target Audience:

iPhone 15: iOS ecosystem users and ardent Apple supporters.

Photographers and videographers on the move looking for exceptional quality.

Users who value efficiency and a seamless user experience. Those seeking a high-end style and level of craftsmanship.

Samsung Galaxy S24: a device for fans of personalization and Android.

Cost-conscious consumers looking for powerful specifications at a reasonable price.

consumers who value attributes like extended battery life and a better display.

Users who prioritize efficiency and multitasking will find benefits in features like Dex desktop mode and expandable storage.

Conclusion

Friends, brick phones are a thing of the past. These days, we can buy pizza at three in the morning and take pictures of Saturn's rings with pocket-sized rockets. The newest players in this electronic race, the iPhone 15 and Galaxy S24 are putting down their hats like digital gunslingers.

The iPhone 15 hints softly of Apple's walled garden, where every element works together like a well-rehearsed dance routine. Conversely, the Galaxy S24 unlocks Android's saloon doors and lets you personalize your phone like a Harley with extra features.

Hey, this isn't a gunfight. These two phones are loaded with power and intelligence. They are portals to universes of information, creativity, and relationships rather than only being devices. Who then prevails? Not some boner with a star rating for tech reviews. When you turn on your phone and embrace your inner rebel, you are the true winner.

Smartphones have as much of a future as the Texas sky. What matters is how you use your phone, not whatever one you select. Now take out your digital six-shooter, choose your path, and pen your darn chapter in this technological epic. The wildest invention, after all, isn't found in silicon—rather, it's found in the hearts of all tech-savvy cowboys. Go ride 'em now, buddy!

This iteration seeks to be more engaging and less formal by:

Employing colloquial jargon and metaphors such as "digital gunslingers" and "pocket-sized rockets."

Adding quips such as "tech reviewer with a star-rating boner" and "perfectly choreographed dance routine" to inject comedy.

Using phrases like "grab your digital six-shooter" and "digital outlaw" to evoke a spirit of strength and adventure.

Establishing a lighthearted and friendly atmosphere with a Western vibe.

So with this guide about the 2 major smartphones, we hope you do make the best choice and start living your digital life!

www.ingramcontent.com/pod-product-compliance
Lightning Source LLC
LaVergne TN
LVHW010040070326
832903LV00071B/4459